Juicing Recipes Book For Vitality, Energy, Health And Fitness Nutrition 14 Healthy Clean Eating & Drinking Juice Cleanse Recipes

Juliana Baltimoore

Published by InfinitYou, 2017.

While every precaution has been taken in the preparation of this book, the publisher assumes no responsibility for errors or omissions, or for damages resulting from the use of the information contained herein.

JUICING RECIPES BOOK FOR VITALITY, ENERGY, HEALTH AND FITNESS NUTRITION 14 HEALTHY CLEAN EATING & DRINKING JUICE CLEANSE RECIPES

First edition. July 12, 2017.

Copyright © 2017 Juliana Baltimoore.

ISBN: 978-1386397403

Written by Juliana Baltimoore.

Juicing For Vitality

T	V	Q	Y	Q	X	N	U	A	F	Q	K	U	H
W	B	E	E	T	P	I	N	E	A	P	P	L	E
L	M	I	P	P	N	G	A	R	L	I	C	V	O
L	A	N	R	A	D	I	S	H	A	J	N	P	V
B	L	Y	L	A	I	N	D	K	A	L	E	P	B
P	W	R	S	P	I	N	A	C	H	J	J	E	K
M	U	E	U	S	N	A	P	P	L	E	O	R	I
E	O	X	U	E	R	K	M	J	E	M	L	Q	N
I	G	G	L	E	M	O	N	N	P	O	F	M	M
T	C	A	R	R	O	T	S	L	M	A	R	R	P
M	G	I	N	G	E	R	Q	B	I	A	A	M	Q
E	J	A	K	S	T	O	M	A	T	O	E	D	E
R	A	S	P	E	R	R	I	E	S	D	R	W	Y
Y	C	D	M	M	Q	T	U	Y	X	V	W	F	A

And Energy

1 handful of kale
2 handful of baby spinach
6 stalks of celery
3 spray of parsley
1 lemon
1 lime
1/2 bulb of fennel
1 beet
3 carrots
1 juicy apple
1 small cucumber

1 beet
4 carrots
1 cup of strawberries
1 cup of rasperries
1 handfull of baby spinach
3 small cucumbers
1 piece of ginger
1 big slice fo pineapple

- 1 Apple
- 5 Carrots
- 1 Beet
- 1 Cucumber
- 1 Black radish

2 small zucchini
2 red apples
4 green or purple kale leaves
4 white or purple cauliflower florets
1 cup blueberries
1 orange
1/2 medium cucumber
Shredded coconut

Introduction

"The word juicing scares people because they think that drinking liquid is dieting. What they don't realize, is that they are regenerating their blood, cells, and organs to live a longer fulfulling life."

Welcome to the wonderful world of juicing!

Thank you for purchasing my juicing book that not only helped me in assoociatiation with drinking smoothies to lose 40 lbs over two month, but I gained many other things from such a lifestyle change.

Since I have been changing my lifestyle to integrate juices in combination with smoothies into my lifestyle and since I have made a habit out of drinking juices and smoothies on a daily basis, I have been able to boost up my vitality, energy & health in general.

This is also the reason why I wrote a second book in my juicing book series. The first concentrates more on the aspect of juices in relation to weight loss and this second one is focused on juicing recipes for vitality, energy & health.

I am consuming my juices and smoothies on a daily basis and I have never been feeling more energized, stress free and fit.

I am going to share my positive health experiences with juicing in this book.

If your goal is to live a more healthy and clean lifestyle to double your life and boost up your health, these are the recipes that you should be consuming on a daily basis.

Make sure to consume a combination of healthy smoothies and juices on a daily basis. This combination strategy is what helped me in the end become successful with my goal (increase my vitality and energy). Combining juices and smoothies also provides you with more different types of healthy drink variations which makes the whole process more fun and exciting.

You can also check out my Smoothies series at the end of this book in order to create your own collection of drink variations.

Just one last tip before we get started with the actual recipes.

These healthy ingredients and nutrients that are inside these juices do even become more beneficial to your body and mind if used and consumed in combination with a light yoga workout or any other workout that you prefer.

Before getting started with my daily juicing and smoothie ritual I had some serious health issues like breathing problems and asthma, stress and sleeping problems, but since I included daily Yoga combined with these healthy juices and smoothies, I am a new person.

Feeling sick is an experience of my past.

I am so happy that I got started with changing my lifestyle from a common and unhealthy meal plan to one that includes these delicious and healthy juices which kind of transformed my life into a balanced, healthy, energized and clean lifestyle!

I am enjoying this lifestyle so much that I decided to motivate and encourage others to get started with juicing for health benefits, too.

Depending on your own goals and preferences, you can either consume juices to become a healthier you or you can apply them as a juicing diet or a combination of juicing and smoothie diet in order to develop a leaner body or to lose some pounds. The first book in this series concentrates more on the weight loss aspects of juicing.

Make sure to first consult your doctor or physician to make sure that this diet is a good fit for your own personal situation.

Preparing these healthy juices with pulp does not take much time out of your schedule, and if you'd like to learn some cool time management tricks that apply to a healthy lifestyle that includes disciplines like yoga and/or meditation then I highly recommend my sister's book series that you can find on the marketplace as well.

Each juicing recipe for weight loss includes a list of ingredients that you need to have in order to get started. Each healthy juice recipe does not take longer than 5 minute in terms of preparation.

For each juice recipe, simply follow my 5 Minute 6 Step Juicing System chapter and make sure to use organic products, fruits and vegetables whenever you can.

I hope you enjoy the book and I hope that you will get lots of inspiration and stimulation out of the book in order to be able to take advantage and be empowered by the fact that these healthy juices are helping you tap into some very powerful health benefits.

Remember, each and every recipe and ingredient has its own healthy benefits!

All you have to do is identify your goal and take your daily action steps. If you follow my juicing for vitality and energy ritual from this book, you will have the same success with these delicious and healthy juices.

If you are looking to become healthier, make sure to integrate more and more of these juice recipes into your daily meal plan.

Everybody has a different goal and you can consume more or less of these juices depending on your personal situation, your goal and your

lifestyle.

One thing is for sure, if you get yourself into the habit of consuming these juices, you will empower and transform your body and mind with the result of a healthier, fitter, cleaner, more vital and more energized you!

My Favorite Quote

"Juices of fruits and vegetables are pure gifts from Mother Nature and the most natural way to heal your body and make yourself whole again." — Farnoosh Brock

Why You Should Read This Book

Juicing is beneficial to your health, but what if you're looking to juice for a specific health benefit? Find and choose the benefit you're looking to juice for below!

Applying a daily juicing ritual will help with the following:

Vitality
Energy
Weight Loss
Natural Beauty & Skin Care
Protection & Healing
Antioxidants
Alzheimer's Prevention
Asthma Help (I suffered for years from breathing problems and Asthma and finally was able to get rid of it because of my daily Juicing and Smoothie ritual)
Blood Cleanse
Arthritis Prevention
Respiration & Asthma Relief
Bone Protection
Cancer Prevention
Cervical Cancer Prevention
Breast Cancer Prevention
Colon Cancer Prevention
Liver Cancer Prevention
Lung Cancer Prevention
Prostate Cancer Prevention
Cataracts Prevention
Ovarian Cancer Prevention
Stomach Cancer Prevention
Digestion
Detoxification
Digestion
Heart Disease Prevention
Immune System
Hydration

Improving Eyesight
Improved Complexion
Increased Blood Circulation
Kidney Cleanse
Increased Libido
Liver Cleanse
Lower Blood Pressure
Lower Cholesterol
Macular Degeneration Prevention
Mental Health
Osteoporosis Prevention
Pain Relief
Reduce Inflammation
Reduce Water Retention
Stroke Prevention

More Benefits From Applying A Daily Juicing Habit:

Increase in energy and alertness as well as a renewed sense overall health and vigor

When you lean the art of juicing you can enjoy delicious and freshly made fruit and veggie juices to boost your system

Enjoy drinking morning boosting juices to get your day started and to be ready to face new challenges

Play with all kinds of flavors and combinations of ingredients in order to find the one combination that you simply can not live without anymore

You can say no to sick making preservatives, chemicals, additives, and yes to natural sweeteners and a wonderful flavor experience

Discover all kinds of juices that you can make and use for other things like:

Freezing your own juices for later usage

Use your homemade juices for your own self-made cooking and baking recipes like pies, breads, soups, sauces, muffins, cakes and many other delicious treats

The juice makes an excellent stock or natural source of sweetener and they are much easier for the body to process than refined sugars

When you really put your mind to juicing, I imagine you will be amazed by all the wonderful uses you can find with these magical, healthy and healing juices

Welcome to the wonderful and magical world of juicing!

The 5 Minute 6 Step Juicing System

Step by Step Instructions For Juicing

For all these juicing recipe simply follow my 5 minute step by step instructions.

Step 1

Wash all veggies and fruits. Going through this thorough cleaning process will help prevent a nasty food-borne disease. I love to use organic vinegar because it is the most natural and organic solution, buy there are other options available if you prefer using products that are specifically designed for washing vegetables and fruits.

Step 2

Peel and cut all your fruits and veggies. Remember, you are juicing raw vegetables. This is why you need to cut them into small pieces before you get started. Especially if you are applying crunchier fruits and veggies such as carrots. Some high speed or high power juicers or a combination of juicer/blender like the Vitamix are able to take veggies and fruits in their whole form. In this case just follow the manufacturer's manual. Peel the skin of all your veggies and fruits. You also need to peel fruits like apples, melons, bananas, papaya, mango, pineapple, kiwis, banans, avocados, etc.

Next cut and chop the fruits and veggies such as leafy greens and fruits.

Step 3

Put your fruits and veggies into your favorite juicer or blender or a combination of juicer/blender (Nutribullet) and strictly follow the directions of the manual that comes with your machine. The manual will tell you what buttons to puch and what speed to use.

Juice the softer fruits/textures first.

You will see that when you are juicing the crunchier veggies and fruits they will help you push the softer and more delicate fruits and veggies through the blades.

If you are not using a juicer and only have a blender available, make sure to first strain the juice from citrus fruits like oranges, lemons, grapefruit, etc. When you are finished you can either leave the pulp inside the juice or take it out. It is totally up to your preference.

Next add the juice back to your mixture in the blender and proceed from there.

Step 4:

Juice and blend everything together as per instructions from your manual. You can always add some raw honey or sweatener depending on your goal with these juices. If the juice is too strong for you, you might also add some ice cubes or source water.

I only add ice cubes and water to smoothies, but some friends of mine who got started with juicing told me that some of the juices were too strong for them and they added ice cubes or water. In the summer time, ice cubes might be a refreshing alternative.

You will see that experimenting with your juicing process will help you discover many varieties and alternatives which makes juicing such a fun and exciting experience.

Step 5:

Try a variety of fruit and vegetable mixtures. As you experiment with juicing, you will find many combinations that you will enjoy on a daily basis. Some that pair well include apples with carrots, and leafy greens with kiwi. Try anything you want to taste. Create several go to recipes for yourself that you can use to make a healthy habit out of juicing.

Step 6:

The last step is a very important one if you want to enjoy your juicer/blender for a very long time.

Make sure to clean your machine ASAP and once you are done with your juice.

This helps prevent nasty bacteria growth and in order to prevent any diseases that related to hygiene.

Use warm water and dish soap. You can also use vinegar to clean and then run the pieces through the dishwasher.

If you do not have a dishwahser take extra care with the cleaning process.

Step 7:

Make sure to add lots of fiber to your smoothies, eat whole fruits and veggies throughout the day in order to stay balanced otherwise you might risk a dietary deficiency.

Step 8:

Enjoy your refreshing and delicious juice and get you day started with lots of vitality and energy...

Step 9:

Refer to chapter Juicing For Vitality & Energy to learn some more intriguing aspects that you can apply to your juicing lifestyle! The goal here is to keep the doctor away and reduce medical bills to ZERO cost and to double your life! (real money and time savers!)

Secret Morning Elixir To Start Your Day With Vitality & Energy

With a consumption of these detoxing and healthy juicing recipes, I was finally able to to rebooted my system.

I am respecting my daily juicing ritual because it provides me with lots of energy and vitality. It is not hard anymore like it was when I first got started.

The secret to a healthy body with lots of energy and vitality is to get started with juicing and to apply this secret morning elexir on a daily basis.

Here is my secret lemon morning elixir that I drink every morning before I have my first juice.

Ingredients:

1 cup of warm or room temperature source water
Juice from 1 lemon (organic if possible)
1 teaspoon of raw apple cider vinegar
A pinch of cinnamon
1 teaspoon of raw honey (alternatively you can also use a couple drops of stevia)

For example, you can use stevia if you are on a yeast cleansing diet or low sugar diet.

I drink this every morning, whether I am "feasting" or not, this is my morning coffee and I enjoy my morning elexir ritual!

What this morning elexir ritual does for you:

This morning elexir stimulates digestion and it releases toxins from the liver. It also jump starts your digestive enzymes.

Benefits of this morning lemon elexir ritual:
Raw honey benefits:

* Raw honey is loaded with minerals, vitamins & enzymes

* It helps cleanse your liver, flushes out fat from your body when done first thing in the morning on an empty stomach and remove toxins

* Raw honey soothes indigestion (it relieves acidity in your stomach)

* Energy booster

* Anti microbial and anti fungal

* Raw honey helps to keep your skin clear (it helps with skin conditions such as ring worms, eczema & psoriasis)

Apple Cider benefits:

* Apple Cider is a natural remedy for heartburn
* It can help clear up your skin conditions and acne
* It promotes digestion and apple cider will keep you regular
* Apple cider helps control weight
* It can help regulate your blood sugar
* Apple Cider helps reduce sinus infections and sore throats
* It is very rich in potassium and enzymes
* It can help ease menstrual cramps
* It also helps promote youthful healthy bodies and skin

Lemon benefits:

* Lemon helps make the body more alkaline (increases pH)

* It provides lots of Vitamin C

* It purifies your blood and detoxes you

* Lemon is a cleansing agent & tonic for your liver by helping it produce more bile

Strawberry Carrot Beautifier

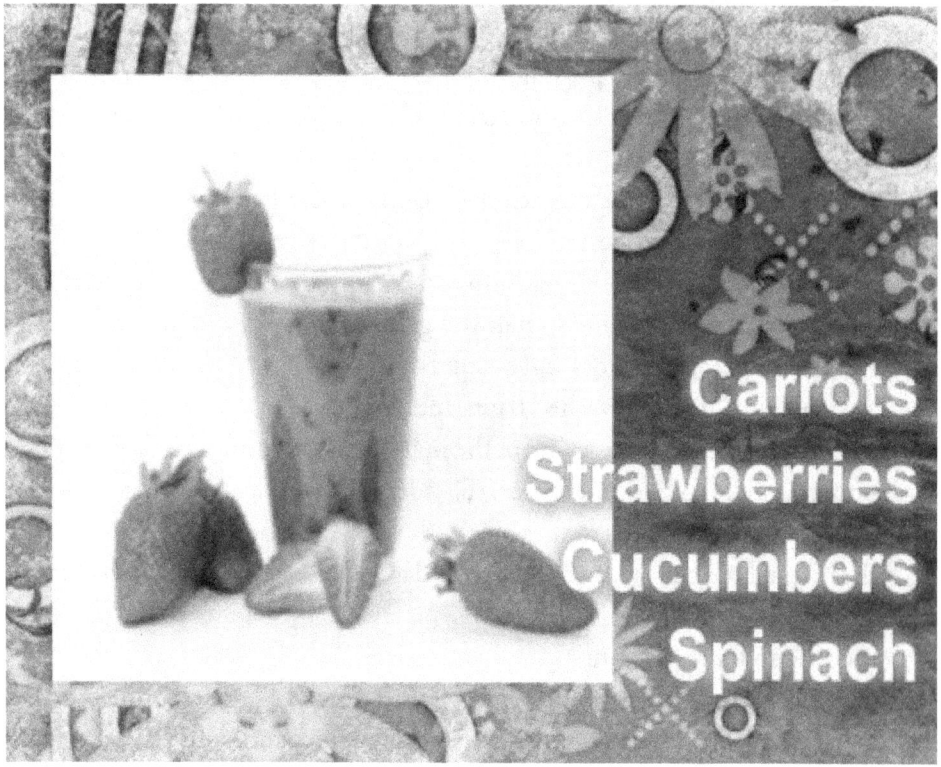

If developing your natural beauty is goal number one for you, this juice is a must! If you want to beautify yourself naturally, make sure to put the Strawberry Carrot Beautifier on your daily juice consumption list.

Pouring the contents of delightful strawberries and organic carrots or baby carrots into my favorite blender (in my case I am using the Nutribullet because it juices and keeps the pulp in the glass plus it also makes my favorite smoothiesn too) and whipping everything together into a zesty healthy natural beauty elexir is my second action every morning and I get my day started most of the times with this beauty drink. First I drink my Secret Morning Elexir and then I continue with my favorite drink that makes me beautiful in a natural way.

This powerful beautifying Juice contains the following ingredients:

Ingredients:

    8 medium to large organic carrots

    10 strawberries (organic if possible)

    3 cucumbers (organic if possible)

    2 large handfuls of spinach (or baby spinach and organic if possible)

Directions:

For the directions please refer to the chapter where I am talking about my 5 Minute 6 Step Juicing System.

Here is a short instruction that sums up what to do. Make sure to refer back to my 6 step process for juicing so that you get the whole idea of juicing.

In this case peel the carrots and cucumbers.

Next cut and chop the washed fruits and veggies.

Put all the fruits and veggies from the ingredients list into your favorite juicer or blender or a combination of juicer/blender (Nutribullet) and strictly follow the directions of the manual that comes with your machine.

The manual of your favorite juicer/blender will tell you what buttons to push and what speed to use.

Juice the softer textures first.

You will see that when you are juicing the crunchier veggies and fruits they will help you push the softer and more delicate fruits and veggies through the blades.

Juice and blend the all the ingredients together as per instructions.

You can always add some raw honey or sweatener depending on your goal with these juices. If the juice is too strong for you, you might also add some ice cubes or source water.

Enjoy your refreshing and delicious Powerful Strawberry Carrot Beautifier!

Lime Lemon Jalapeno Ginger Gold

This is my favorite citrus tonic drink and I make sure to mix it into my daily meal plan because it helped me control my Asthma and breathing problems.

The secret combination of limes and lemons is what makes this juice a Vitamin C booster. It is a is also a great liver detoxifier.

In a condition of insufficient oxygen and breathing problems (mountain climbing, etc.) lemons are very helpful.

I suffered from Asthma and breating problems and have been able to get rid of it by changing by eating and drinking habits. Drinking this juice is part of my daily juicing ritual.

Vitamin C in lemons for example helps the body to neutralize free radicals that are linked to most types of diseases and aging.

The added health benefits of the ginger and the other ingredients are making this health exexir a vitality bomb!

This Lime Lemon Jalapeno Ginger Gold Elexir is a winner and it contains the following ingredients:

Ingredients:

2 Lemons with Skin and only if organic

1 Lime with skin and only if organic

10 Ribs of Celery (organic if possible)

2 inch of Fresh Ginger (organic if possible)

2 cups of Parsley (organic if possible)

2 Apples (any kind and organic if possible)

1/2 Jalapeno (this is a hot ingredient so be careful)

Alternative to the Jalapeno:

Sprinkle some cayenne pepper on top of your tonic drink when it's finished!

Directions:

For the directions please refer to the chapter where I am talking about my 5 Minute 6 Step Juicing System.

Here is a short instruction that sums up what to do. Make sure to refer back to my 6 step process for juicing so that you get the whole idea of juicing.

In this case peel the ginger and the apples.

Next cut and chop the thoroughly washed veggies and fruits.

Put your ingredients into your favorite juicer or blender or a combination of juicer/blender (Nutribullet) and strictly follow the directions of the manual that comes with your machine.

Your blender manual will tell you what buttons to push and what speed to use.

Juice the softer textures first.

You will see that when you are juicing the crunchier veggies and fruits they will help you push the softer and more delicate fruits and veggies through the blades.

If you are not using a juicer and only have a blender available, make sure to first strain the juice from the lime and lemons.

Once it is finished you can either leave the pulp inside or take it out. This is totally up to your preference.

In this case you have to add the juices back to the blender and proceed from there.

Juice and blend the juice with the rest of your ingredients together as per instructions.

You can always add some raw honey or sweatener depending on your goal with these juices. If the juice is too strong for you, you might also add some ice cubes or source water.

Enjoy this Vitamine C enriched delicious tonic!

Grapefruit Cranberry Double Immune System Blaster

- 8 Apples
- 10-12 carrots
- 1 bunch of celery
- 2 oranges
- 2 grapefruit
- 1 pound of fresh cranberries
- 5" or 6" piece of fresh ginger

A combination of healthy superfood type of ingredients: cranberries and ginger is what this smoothie is all about. The Grapefruit Cranberry Double Immune System Blaster is a perfect solution if your goal is to follow a healthy and clean juicing lifestyle.

So what is so beneficial about juicing cranberries? Consuming cranberries in their natural form (not buying cranberry juices with added sugar) has the following health benefits:

Cranberries are a protection against Urinary Tract Infection (UTI), they give anti-inflammatory benefits, cardiovascular benefits, antioxidant protection, as well as anti-cancer benefits.

The intake of cranberry extracts has shown the ability to improve multiple aspects of immune functions and it has shown the abillity to lower the frequency of cold and flu symptoms.

Cranberries in combination with ingredients like ginger are even more powerful.

What makes the ginger so powerful in terms of health benefits?

The anti inflammatory properties and active principles of the ginger root are thought to provide pain relief in multiple number of ways. It has the power to stop migraines in their tracks and to ease the aches of arthritis and joint pain.

It also fights ovarian cancer. It seems that ginger has the ability to eliminate the dangerous cancerous ovarian cells. Ginger also seems to slow the progress of bowel cancer.

Ginger also has a boosting effect on the immune system, making you fit and healthy.

Make sure to consume this immune system boosting smoothie drink on a daily basis to stay healthy and clean all year around!

I suggest to drink this juice in slow sips and you can keep it near your workspace so you can take a sip throughout the day.

Ginger also improves your breath. It can cleanse the palate leaving your mouth feeling refreshed.

Ginger protects against nuclear radiation and if you want to get the full benefits of this advantage you will have to consume a daily dose.

Ginger also strengthens your immunity. An improved immune system can mean that you get ill less often. It means that you will recover quicker. It also means that when everyone else around you is coming down with something you can stay fit and healthy.

Ginger also fights cancers. Ginger has been shown to help treat various forms of cancer, including ovarian cancer.

Ginger protects against Alzheimer's disease.

Ginger helps to slow down the loss of brain cells that typically is the precursor to Alzheimer's disease.

Ginger is perfect for weight loss because it stimulates the appetite. If you have a very sluggish digestive system and find out that you need to get your digestive fire going before eating a meal, ginger can help you out.

Ginger can also help as an appetite stimulant to get your digestive juices flowing so that you are better able to digest foods and lose weight as a side effect because improper digestion of food leaves the food fermenting in your digestive system which can lead to weight gain as a side effect.

Ginger is a fat burning superfood and it acts as a fat burner. Ginger helps you feel satisfied and full. This means that you will eat less food which will help reducing your overall caloric intake in the end.

Ginger is a true magical secret ingredient and this juice combines ginger and turns it into an even healthier raw power cocktail.

I am enjoying the benefits of ginger every day. If I do not have enough time to make a juice because I am pressed in time, I consume at least a glass of ginger water or ginger tea with lemon.

If you are looking to lose weight like I did, you make sure to drink a glass of this magical ginger water or ginger/lemon water (cold or hot as herbal tea) throughout the day and in little sips. If you apply this ginger water method you will always feel full and satisfied.

I have tested this juice with a lot of friends and family members before adding it to my favorite collection of juices. They all got some great benefits out of drinking this health elexir on a daily basis.

I am constantly testing and proving new juicing recipes that I am gradually adding to my "Tested & Proven Juicing Recipe Collection"

This one has passed the test because it is not only delicious, but it is such a healthy treat.

Celery might not sound appealing to you at first, but the combination of all the ingredients is turning this juice into an absolute winner. It does not only taste deliciously, but it provides your body and brain with a powerful mix of rejuvenating and healing nutrition.

This healthy elexir called the Grapefruit Cranberry Double Immune System Blaster contains the following ingredients:

Ingredients:
8 Apples (organic if possible)
10-12 carrots or baby carrots (organic if possible)
1 bunch of celery (organic if possible)
2 oranges (for juicing and organic if possible)
2 grapefruit (organic if possible)

1 pound of fresh cranberries (frozen are ok if you can't find fresh ones and organic if possible)

5" or 6" piece of fresh ginger (organic if possible)

Alternative Fruits:

You can also add pears, melons, grapes, whatever the season and whatever your taste is!

Directions:

For the directions please refer to the chapter where I am talking about my 5 Minute 6 Step Juicing System.

Here is a short instruction that sums up what to do. Make sure to refer back to my 6 step process for juicing so that you get the whole idea of juicing.

In this case peel the apples, carrots oranges, grapefruits and ginger.

Next cut and chop the fruits and veggies.

Put all the fruits and veggies from the ingredients list into your favorite juicer or blender or a combination of juicer/blender (Nutribullet) and strictly follow the directions of the manual that comes with your machine.

Your blender manual will tell you what buttons to push and what speed to use.

Juice the softer textures first.

You will see that when you are juicing the crunchier veggies and fruits they will help you push the softer and more delicate fruits and veggies through the blades.

If you are not using a juicer and only have a blender available, make sure to first strain the juice from the oranges and the grapefruits first.

Once it is finished you can either leave the pulp inside or take it out. This is totally up to your preference.

In this case you have to add the juice back to the blender and proceed from there.

Juice and blend the juice with all the other ingredients together as per instructions.

You can always add some raw honey or sweatener depending on your goal with these juices. If the juice is too strong for you, you might also add some ice cubes or source water.

Enjoy your refreshing and delicious Grapefruit Cranberry Double Immune System Blaster!

Liquid Tomatoe Booster

This is another one of my natural beauty juices. I make sure to mix it at least 3 to 4 times into my weekly meal plan because I enjoy the beautifying benefits of it. It really makes my skin soft, hydrated and wrinkle free. I apply some powerful organic and self made beauty products to my skin (cocoa butter, apple cider, honey and aloe vera) and like this (juicing + natural self made beauty products) my body is able to stay beautiful from the inside out.

I am working on a new series where I divulge my organic homemade skin care and beauty secrets and you can soon check it out and add these beauty secrets to your own home spa and beauty program, too.

A combination of juices and smoothies, the benefits from my self made beauty and skin care system and a light yoga and meditation workout is all I need in order to create the ultimate healthy lifestyle for myself and my family.

This red beauty juice is a fortified and nutritious combination of vitality boosting superfood reds and greens like tomatoes, kale, lettuce, swiss chard, and romaine.

Mixing nutritious veggies and greens like tomatoes, onions, garlic, kale and all types of different salads will bring an almost sweet taste to this juice because the tomatoe fruits (yes tomatoes are fruits!) help neutralize strong and bitter flavours that might come from the veggies and greens.

The ginger gives this juice drink some powerful health benefits like immune boosting actions.

The reason kale is becoming popular is because it helps you fill up without a lot of calories to speak of. It doesn't have any fat, has plenty of fiber as well as iron and Vitamin K. Because of its antioxidant content you'll get anti-inflammatory benefits which helps to reduce the symptoms of inflammation, while also helping to avoid the rise of certain diseases. It also helps to restore and maintain an alkaline state.

This Liquid Tomatoe Booster contains the following ingredients:

Ingredients:

1 bunch of Romaine lettuce (organic if possible)

6 medium ripe tomatoes (organic if possible)

1 thick slice of Vidalia or other mild onion (about 1/4" thick and organic if possible)

5-6 cloves fresh, peeled garlic (organic if possible)

You can substitute Swiss Chard or Kale for the Romaine (organic if possible)

5" or 6" piece of fresh ginger (organic if possible)

Directions:

For all these For the directions please refer to the chapter where I am talking about my 5 Minute 6 Step Juicing System.

Here is a short instruction that sums up what to do. Make sure to refer back to my 6 step process for juicing so that you get the whole idea of juicing.

In this case peel the tomatoes, the onion, the ginger and the garlic.

Next cut and chop the fruits and veggies.

Put all the fruits and veggies from the ingredients list into your favorite juicer or blender or a combination of juicer/blender (Nutribullet) and strictly follow the directions of the manual that comes with your machine.

Your blender manual will tell you what buttons to push and what speed to use.

Juice the softer textures first.

You will see that when you are juicing the crunchier veggies they will help you push the softer and more delicate veggies through the blades.

Juice and blend all the ingredients from the list above together as per instructions.

If the juice is too strong for you, you might also add some ice cubes or source water.

Enjoy your refreshing Liquid Tomatoe Booster that will beautify and energize you from the inside out!

Double Melon Elexir

If you love tasty juices with some powerful orange and green ingredients that are super healthy and taste deliciously, then you might consider the Double Melon Elexir.

Cantaloupes are a rich source of folates, carotenoids, potassium, and vitamin C.

They grow naturally in Africa and Asia. People eat cantaloupes because of its juicy, tasty flavor. Some people even use it as an appetizer and as an ingredient for salads.

Honeydews are rich in potassium, vitamin C, copper, B vitamins.

One cup of honeydew will provide about half of your daily vitamin C needs. Vitamin C helps boost your immune system which in turn will help prevent infections and illnesses.

Honeydew melons are a member of the melon fruit family. Honeydew melon has pale green juicy and sweet flesh. Honeydew melons are a very nutritious addition for people who are on a diet. Honeydew melons also contain several vitamins and minerals. They only have 60 calories per half cup which makes them a very nutritionally beneficial fruit.

Pouring the contents of a delightful cantaloupe, honeydew, fresh apples, kale and swiss chard into your favorite blender (in my case I am using the Nutribullet because I love its versatillity) and whip it all together into a zesty nutritious rich elexir that heals from the inside out and keeps your body healthy and fit.

This sweet and tasty double melon elixir contains the following ingredients:

Ingredients:
2 Apples (organic if possible)
1/2 Cantaloupe (organic if possible)
1/2 Honeydew (organic if possible)
6-8 leaves Kale (organic if possible)
6-8 leaves Swiss Chard (organic if possible)

Directions:
For the directions please refer to the chapter where I am talking about my 5 Minute 6 Step Juicing System.

Here is a short instruction that sums up what to do. Make sure to refer back to my 6 step process for juicing so that you get the whole idea of juicing.

In this case peel the apples and scrape out the juicy contents of the melons.

Next cut and chop the fruits and veggies.

Put all the fruits and veggies from the ingredients list into your favorite juicer or blender or a combination of juicer/blender (Nutribullet) and strictly follow the directions of the manual that comes with your machine.

The manual will tell you what buttons to push and what speed to use.

Juice the softer textures first.

You will see that when you are juicing the crunchier veggies and fruits they will help you push the softer and more delicate fruits and veggies through the blades.

Juice and blend all the ingredients from the list above together as per instructions.

You can always add some raw honey or sweatener depending on your goal with these juices. If the juice is too strong for you, you might also add some ice cubes or source water.

Enjoy this refreshing and hydrating Double Melon Health Elexir that will beautify and heal you from the inside out!

Zesty Blackberry Ginger Booster

This is a fortified and nutritious combination of healthy and vitality boosting fruits such as grapes and blackberries.

This juice gets its rich flavour from the mix of this powerful combination of fruits.

This dark superfood cocktail also contains the benefits of zesty ginger that is swirled into the juice.

This juice makes for a perfect wholesome and healthy start of your day with lots of energy and vitality.

If you feel that the juice is too strong or too bitter, you can always add another sweet and juicy apple into the blend to make it sweeter in taste.

I enjoy this juice with the contents of at least 2 apples as a breakfast juice and I only use 1 apple if I consume this juice as a lunch or dinner juice. Usually I consume this recipe with only 1 apple instead of coffee after a light lunch meal.

The Zesty Blackberry Ginger Booster contains the following ingredients:

Ingredients:

6 cups of Concord Grapes (any grapes will do and organic if possible)
1 Golden Delicious Apple (organic if possible)
2" piece Ginger (organic if possible)
1/2 cup of Blackberries (organic if possible)

Directions:

For the directions please refer to the chapter where I am talking about my 5 Minute 6 Step Juicing System.

Here is a short instruction that sums up what to do. Make sure to refer back to my 6 step process for juicing so that you get the whole idea of juicing.

In this case peel the apple and ginger.

Next cut and chop the fruits.

Put all the fruits from the ingredients list into your favorite juicer or blender or a combination of juicer/blender (Nutribullet) and strictly follow the directions of the manual that comes with your machine.

Your juicer or blander manual will tell you what buttons to push and what speed to use.

Juice the softer textures first.

You will see that when you are juicing the crunchier fruits they will help you push the softer and more delicate fruits through the blades.

Juice and blend the juices with the other ingredients from the list above together as per instructions.

You can always add some raw honey or sweatener depending on your goal with these juices. If the juice is too strong for you, you might also add some ice cubes or source water.

Enjoy this Blackberry Ginger Tonic and boost your body's vitality!

Blueberry Coconut Veggie Detoxer

2 small zucchini
2 red apples
4 green or purple kale leaves
4 white or purple cauliflower florets
1 cup blueberries
1 orange
1/2 medium cucumber
Shredded coconut

Who says that vegetables are for lunch and dinner only? This leafy green cocktail contains delicious and zesty fruits that are swirled into the greens and this juice makes for a perfect wholesome and healthy start of your day so that you do not need to wait for lunchtime to eat these healthy veggies.

It does not only taste deliciously, but kale provides the body with anti inflammatory health benefits. The Vitamin C of the lemon detoxifies your body and destroys intestinal worms and the cauliflower

There are several dozen studies linking cauliflower containing diets to bladder cancer, breast cancer, colon cancer, prostate cancer, and ovarian cancer prevention.

Cauliflower provides special nutrient support for the detox system, the antioxidant, and the inflammatory/anti-inflammatory system that are connected with cancer prevention and cancer development.

Chronic imbalances in any of these 2 systems of the body can increase the risk of cancer. When imbalances in all of the three systems occur simultaneously, the risk of cancer does increases significantly.

Cauliflower does provide the following health benefits. It gives detox support. It provides the body with antioxidant benefits, it provides ant-inflammatory benefits, it provides the body with cardiovascular support and digestive support.

The zucchini is one of the very low calorie vegetables because it only has 17 calories per 100 g. The zucchini contains no saturated fats or cholesterol. It is a good source of dietary fibers that do help reduce constipation which in turn offers some protection against colon cancer.

Zucchinis have an anti-oxidant value of around 180 Trolex Equivalents (TE) per 100g which is far below some of the superfood berries and vegetables. Nonetheless, the Zucchinis, especially golden skin zucchini varieties, are very rich in flavonoid poly-phenolic antioxidants such as lutein, carotenes, and zeaxanthin. These compounds do help scavenge harmful oxygen-derived free radicals. These compounds also do reactive oxygen species from the body that do play a critical role in the aging process and various other disease processes.

Courgettes which is another word for zucchinis also do have a relative moderate source of folates. Folates are important in cell division and the DNA synthesis. When taken in adequately before a pregnancy, zucchinis can help prevent neural tube defects in the unborn baby.

It is also a very rich source of potassium which is an important intra-cellular electrolyte. Potassium is also a very heart friendly electrolyte and it helps bring the reduction in blood pressure and heart rates.

Fresh zucchinis, indeed, are a rich source of anti oxidant vitamin C.

In addition, zucchinis contain moderate levels of B-complex groups of vitamins like pyridoxine, thiamin, riboflavin as well as minerals like manganese, iron, zinc, and phosphorus.

The coconut is the last secret ingredient of this elexir because the coconut oil that is contained in the coconut is highly beneficial for the health and beauty.

The coconut helps prevent obesity and it improves the heart health. It is high in dietary fiber.

Coconut fiber also slows down the release of glucose and it therefore requires less insulin to utilize the glucose and transports it into the cell. In the cell it is converted into energy.

Coconut assists in relieving stress on the pancreas and enzyme systems of the body. This in turn reduces the risk that is associated with Diabetes.

Coconut reduces sweet cravings and does improve the insulin secretion and the utilization of blood glucose.

The healthy fat in coconut slows down any rise in blood sugar.

The coconut improves digestion and many of the symptoms and inflammatory conditions associated with digestive and bowel disorders.

It is a quick energy boost and provides your body with a quick energy boost - a super nutritious source of extra energy.

Coconut is actually utilized by the body to produce energy, instead of storing it as body fat.

Coconut provides endurance during an athletic or physical performance. It promotes healthy thyroid functions.

Finally, coconut helps to relieve the symptoms of a chronic fatigue and vitalizes the body with a quick energy boost!

If you like the taste of coconut, I highly recommend to keep a glass of fresh coconut water next to you. This keeps you energized during the day in a very natural way!

The highly nutritious Blueberry Coconut Veggie Detoxer contains the following ingredients:

Ingredients:
2 small zucchini (organic if possible)
2 red apples (organic if possible)
4 green kale leaves (organic if possible)
4 white or purple cauliflower florets (organic if possible)
1 1/2 cup blueberries (organic if possible)
1 orange, peeled (use oranges that are best for juicing and never juice citrus fruits with the skin)
1 lemon (peeled and organic if possible)
1/2 medium cucumber (organic if possible)

Shredded coconut (only fresh and for added sweetness and totally optional)

Directions:

For all these juice recipe For the directions please refer to the chapter where I am talking about my 5 Minute 6 Step Juicing System.

Here is a short instruction that sums up what to do. Make sure to refer back to my 6 step process for juicing so that you get the whole idea of juicing.

In this case peel the apples, orange, lemon, and cucumber.

Next cut and chop the fruits and veggies.

Put all the fruits and veggies from the ingredients list into your favorite juicer or blender or a combination of juicer/blender (Nutribullet) and strictly follow the directions of the manual that comes with your machine.

The manual will tell you what buttons to push and what speed to use.

Juice the softer textures first.

You will see that when you are juicing the crunchier veggies and fruits they will help you push the softer and more delicate fruits and veggies through the blades.

If you are not using a juicer and only have a blender available, make sure to first strain the juice from the orange and lemon.

Once it is finished you can either leave the pulp inside or take it out. This is totally up to your preference.

In this case you have to add the juice back to the blender and proceed from there.

Juice and blend the juices with the other ingredients from the list above together as per instructions.

You can always add some raw honey or sweatener depending on your goal with these juices. If the juice is too strong for you, you might also add some ice cubes or source water.

Enjoy this powerful and tasty Blueberry Coconut Veggie Detoxer!

Orange Breakfast Power Cocktail

"Oranges strengthen your emotional body, encouraging a general feeling of joy, well-being, and cheerfulness." - Tae Yun Kim

Let's talk about this simple and yet powerful combination of apples and carrots. The secret of this juice lies in its simplicity.

Let's take a look at what an apple a day can do for you in combination with carrots.

Carrots have lots of health benefits. Carrots help improve the eye visions because carrots are rich in beta-carotene. Beta-Carotene is converted into vitamin A in the liver. Vitamin A is then transformed in the retina.

Some other health benefits are cancer prevention, anti-aging, healthy glowing skin, prevention from infections, beautiful and rejuvenated skin, prevention from heart disease, body cleansing, healthy teeth and gums, and stroke prevention.

Medical studies have shown that carrots help reduce the risk of breast cancer, lung cancer, and colon cancer. Researchers have just discovered falcarindiol and falcarinol which cause the anticancer properties.

The high level of beta carotene acts as an antioxidant to cell damage that is done to the body through regular metabolism. Carrots help slow down the aging of the cells.

Carrots are known to prevent infection. If you cut yourself, try shredded raw or boiled mashed carrots as a natural solution to prevent infections.

Diets that contain a high amount of carotenoids are associated with a lower risk of heart diseases. A regular consumption of carrots also helps minimize the cholesterol levels. The soluble fibers contained in these delicious and crunchy carrots bind with bile acids.

Vitamin A helps the liver in flushing out toxins and waste from the body. It reduces the bile and the fat in the liver. The fibers that are present in the carrots do help clean out the colon.

Crunchy carrots also help clean your mouth and teeth. Carrots scrape off plaque and food particles in a natural way. Carrots stimulate gums and trigger a lot of saliva. The minerals in carrots prevent tooth damage, too.

Crunching carrots or juicing carrots will also help protect against strokes.

Mixing carrot juice together with orange juice becomes even more powerful.

Here is what oranges can do for you. Oranges are nutritional and powerful fruits because they provide an array of health benefits to your body. Oranges have a wealth of nutrients including vitamin A precursors, vitamin C, calcium, potassium, and pectin.

Oranges alkalize the body, protect your skin, help with the regulation of a high blood pressure in the body, help create good eye vision, and relieve constipation.

They are also very effective in fighting against viral infections.

Oranges are very rich in citrus limonoids, which is proven to help fight a number of varieties of cancers, including skin cancer, stomach cancer, lung cancer, breast cancer, stomach cancer, and colon cancer.

They are very effective in fighting against viral infections.

Drinking orange juice regularly reduces the risk of kidney stones and prevents kidney diseases.

Since oranges are full of soluble fiber, oranges are helpful in lowering the cholesterol level. Oranges are also full of potassium, an electrolyte mineral that is responsible for helping the heart function. When these potassium levels go down, you may develop an abnormal heart rhythm.

Lastly, oranges are full of vitamin C which protects your cells by neutralizing free radicals. Free radicals do cause chronic diseases, like heart diseases and cancer.

As you can see carrots and oranges provide lots of powerful health benefit and they taste deliciously, too, and who does not like to enjoy a juicy orange snack or drink or like to crunch tasty carrots with healthy dips

Oranges are very popular with athletes because oranges can be easily taken in for a quick burst of energy.

Apart from drinking this orange carrot juice on a daily basis, I also love eating one or two oranges a day and for that same energy-boosting effects as athletes are doing it.

This Orange Breakfast Power Cocktail contains the following ingredients:

Ingredients:
6 carrots (organic if possible)
2 apples (organic if possible)

Directions:
For all these juice recipe For the directions please refer to the chapter where I am talking about my 5 Minute 6 Step Juicing System.

Here is a short instruction that sums up what to do. Make sure to refer back to my 6 step process for juicing so that you get the whole idea of juicing.

In this case peel the apples and carrots.

Next cut and chop them up.

Put them into your favorite juicer or blender or a combination of juicer/blender (Nutribullet) and strictly follow the directions of the manual that comes with your machine.

The manual will tell you what buttons to puch and what speed to use.

Juice and blend them together as per instructions of your machine's manual.

You can always add some raw honey or sweatener depending on your goal with these juices. If the juice is too strong for you, you might also add some ice cubes or source water.

Enjoy this Orange Breakfast Power Cocktail!

Full Body Detoxer

Are you looking for a full body cleanse and detox? I highly recommend this Green Tonic to wash out all the toxins from your system.

This Green Tonic is for you, if you love juices with some weird secret ingredient combinations that are super effective and that taste deliciously. You can always add a sweet apple if the taste is too strong for you.

Pouring the contents of a delightful juicy apple into your favorite blender and whip it all together into the most effective detox elexir is one of my favorite moments of the week.

This full body detoxer is very strong and I do not like to consume this juice every day. However, I make sure to at least consume this detoxing drink once per week.

If you are following an intensive full body cleanse program, this type of juice is what you want to aim for.

This drink cleanses your system so that your body functions are going to work more productively after this strong elexir. It flushes out water, waste and toxins and helps boost up your system.

The full body detoxer contains the following ingredients:

Ingredients:
  3 ribs of celery (organic if possible)
  1 big handful of spinach (organic if possible or organic baby spinach)
  2 stalks of asparagus (organic if possible)
  1 large tomato (organic if possible)
  1 carrot (organic if possible)

Directions:

For all these juice recipe For the directions please refer to the chapter where I am talking about my 5 Minute 6 Step Juicing System.

Here is a short instruction that sums up what to do. Make sure to refer back to my 6 step process for juicing so that you get the whole idea of juicing.

In this case peel the tomatoe, carrot and the aspargus.

Next cut and chop the veggies.

Put all the fruits and veggies from the ingredients list into your favorite juicer or blender or a combination of juicer/blender (Nutribullet) and strictly follow the directions of the manual that comes with your machine.

Your blender manual will tell you what buttons to push and what speed to use.

Juice the softer textures first.

You will see that when you are juicing the crunchier veggies they will help you push the softer and more delicate ones through the blades.

Juice and blend all the ingredients from the list above together as per instructions.

Enjoy the Full Body Detoxer!

Green Gold Juice

The ingredients of this powerful juice are all very beneficial for the body and brain.

Spinach is one of the most nutrient dense packed foods you can provide your body with. It proves you with energy. Spinach helps you fill your stomach without adding a lot of calories and you feel satisfied and full.

Spinach contains phytonutrients that are working as antioxidants battling against the free radical damage.

By consuming spinach you are helping to nourish your body on a cellular level.

Spinach is a great ingredinet for weight loss juices.

Spinach is also an alkaline powerhouse. Baby spinach is great, too. Since there are so many other alkalizing vegetables out there, I recommend trying out different variations and concoct a juice that will send your pH levels to the sky.

This is also the reason why I love combining spinach and kale or baby spinach with spinach and kale.

The health benefits of celery are very powerful, too. In addition to being an alkaline food, celery is very low in calories and it is a great weight loss ingredient for juicing if weight loss is on your mind.

Celery is a great combination as a third ingredient because it brings even more health benefits to the table.

I always love to add celery into fruit based juices as well because it adds a bit of spiciness without overshadowing the sweet flavors of the fruits.

Experimenting with and knowing the benefits of all these ingredients is key to a successful juicing experience.

Parsley is the third green raw ingredient that powers up this juice drink to the next level. Parsley also helps keep your body alkaline. This green herb is not only powering up your juice with lots of health nutrients, but it helps bring out the freshest taste ever. It freshes up the taste of your juice because it adds more vitamins and minerals to your juice.

The great thing is that you can grow your own parsley pretty easily at home and always have it ready to freshen up your juices, smoothies and other recipes that you are making.

I only grow my own parsley and include it in most of my juicing drinks.

The fourth green ingredient of this power packed juice is the cucumber. The cucumber is a heavy hitter. I always keep a good stock of cucumbers at home. Cucumbers are alkaline, and they do contain so much water that it is a very hydrating vegetable.

The radish is very rich in folic acids and Vitamine C and even anthocyanins. These nutrients make the radish a very effective fighting food against cancer. Radish is effective in fighting oral cancer, intestinal cancer and colon cancer as well as stomach and kidney cancers.

Radishes also do contain Zinc, Vitamine C, and B-complex vitamins and phosphorus which is effective in treating skin disorders such as dry skin and rashes.

Radish juices are good for your digestive system and soothes it. Radish is a powerful detoxer and cleans your entire body from toxins. It helps to relieve the congestions's of the respiratory system, too.

Radish juice is an excellent ingredinet for asthmatic individual. People who are suffering from sinus and/or bronchial infections should tap into the healing power of radish.

It is beneficial for both the liver functions and the gallbladder because it acts as a cleaning agent.

Radish also contains sulphur based chemicals. This helps regulate the production and the flow of bile and bilirubin, acids and enzymes.

It also helps get rid of the excess bilirubin contained in the blood. Radish acts as a powerful detoxifying agent for your entire body.

Lastly, radish is highly effective in treating jaundice. Radish is able to halt the destruction of the red blood cells while increasing the supply of the blood's oxygen.

I highly recommend to use black radish for treating jaundice because it is stronger.

Radish is also a natural diuretic. It is very effective in fighting and preventing urinary tract infections. Radish juices do help to cure the burning feeling of the urinary tract. It helps heal bladder infections because it is the perfect natural kidney cleanser.

As you can see this juicing drink is a loaded with powerful ingredients that you can mix up and find lots of variations that might work for you.

I like adding some zesty ginger, orange and lemon to this power cocktail which makes the bitter taste of the celery and radish sweeter and like this you can transform it into the perfect healthy morning and breakfast booster.

The Green Gold Juice contains the following ingredients:

Ingredients:
4 Stalks of celery (organic if possible)
1 Cup of Spinach or baby spinach (organic if possible)
2 Cucumber (organic if possible)
1 Orange (organic if possible)
A few sprigs of parsley (organic if possible)
1 small knob of ginger (organic if possible)
1 small radish (organic if possible)
1 lemon (organic if possible)
1 big slice of pineapple
Directions:

For all these juice recipe For the directions please refer to the chapter where I am talking about my 5 Minute 6 Step Juicing System.

Here is a short instruction that sums up what to do. Make sure to refer back to my 6 step process for juicing so that you get the whole idea of juicing.

In this case peel the radish, pineapple, ginger, orange, lemon, and cucumber.

Next cut and chop the fruits and veggies.

Put all the fruits and veggies from the ingredients list into your favorite juicer or blender or a combination of juicer/blender (Nutribullet) and strictly follow the directions of the manual that comes with your machine.

The manual will tell you what buttons to push and what speed to use.

Juice the softer textures first.

You will see that when you are juicing the crunchier veggies and fruits they will help you push the softer and more delicate fruits and veggies through the blades.

If you are not using a juicer and only have a blender available, make sure to first strain the juice from the lemon and orange.

Once it is finished you can either leave the pulp inside or take it out. This is totally up to your preference.

In this case you have to add the juice back to the blender and proceed from there.

Juice and blend the juices with the other ingredients from the list above together as per instructions.

You can always add some raw honey or sweatener depending on your goal with these juices. If the juice is too strong for you, you might also add some ice cubes or source water.

Enjoy your Green Gold Juice!

Beet & Black Radish Liver Cleanser

1 Apple
5 Carrots
1 Beet
1 Cucumber
1 Black radish

This beetroot liver cleanser contains a combination of healthy and cleansing cucumbers, beets, black radish and carrots. The secret of this juice comes from the combination.

The beets, carrots and cucumber are all nutrient-rich and packed with antioxidants and this is what makes this juice so powerful. This drink is a true immune system booster. It also is a powerful liver cleanse and detox drink because it cleans your system and makes it toxin free.

Beets provide the body with a rich source of Vitamin C and a wide range of other health benefits. The beetroot also contains folate and this helps prevent cancer and heart diseases.

The carrots enhance your vision health. Carrots provide you with a rich supply of antioxidant nutrients called beta carotene.

Cucumbers contain so much water that it is a very hydrating vegetable which combines very well with the healing benefits of the beet and the carrots.

Lastly, radish is highly effective in treating jaundice. Radish is able to halt the destruction of the red blood cells while increasing the supply of the blood's oxygen.

This hydrating liver cleanser juice is the perfect power booster for hot summer days, in the morning and whenever your body needs a good supply of hydratation and the Beet & Black Radish Liver Cleanser contains the following ingredients:

Ingredients:
1 Apple (organic if possible)
5 carrots (organic if possible)
1 beet (organic if possible)
1 cucumber (organic if possible)
1 black radish (organic if possible)

Directions:
For the directions please refer to the chapter where I am talking about my 5 Minute 6 Step Juicing System.

Here is a short instruction that sums up what to do. Make sure to refer back to my 6 step process for juicing so that you get the whole idea of juicing.

In this case peel the apple, the radish, the beets (or buy them already prepared and ready to use), carrots and cucumber.

Next cut and chop the veggies.

Put all the veggies from the ingredients list into your favorite juicer or blender or a combination of juicer/blender (Nutribullet) and strictly follow the directions of the manual that comes with your machine.

The manual will tell you what buttons to push and what speed to use.

Juice the softer textures first. You will see that when you are juicing the crunchier fruits and veggies first they will help you push the softer and more delicate ones through the blades.

Juice and blend all the ingredients from the list above together as per instructions.

Enjoy this refreshing and hydrating Beet and Black Radish Liver Cleanser!

Exotic Strawberry Rasperry Vitality Drink

1 beet
4 carrots
1 cup of strawberries
1 cup of rasperries
1 handfull of baby spinach
3 small cucumbers
1 piece of ginger
1 big slice fo pineapple

Let's talk about a powerful combination of some fortified and nutritious red/orange superfoods like carrots, beets, strawberries and green superfoods.

The secret of this juice is the combination of the red/orange superfoods together with the greens.

This is a magical mixture of orange and green nutritious and healing vegetables and fruits. These are ingredients that do not only taste deliciously, but they will also give your body and brain the most powerful health benefits.

Carrots have a rich supply of antioxidant nutrients called beta carotene.

These delicious orange vegetables are the source not only of beta carotene, but also of a wide variety of antioxidants plus other health supporting nutrients.

Other benefits of carrots are antioxidant benefits, cardiovascular benefits and vision for your health.

The real benefit of strawberris is that they are tasting great and that they are providing enough nutrients to the body.

Strawberries provide a boost to your immune system. They helps your eyes and they help fight cancer. They also helps with cholesterol and with inflammation. They also have anti-aging properties.

The mix of greens combined with orange and red raw fruits and veggies is what makes this juice so special.

The Exotic Strawberry Rasperry Vitality & Energy Booster contains the following ingredients:

Ingredients:

1 beet (organic if possible)
4 carrots (organic if possible)
1 cup of strawberries (organic if possible)
1 cup of rasperries (organic if possible)
1 handfull of baby spinach (organic if possible)
3 small cucumbers (organic if possible)
1 piece of ginger
1 big slice fo pineapple

Directions:

For all these juice recipe For the directions please refer to the chapter where I am talking about my 5 Minute 6 Step Juicing System.

Here is a short instruction that sums up what to do. Make sure to refer back to my 6 step process for juicing so that you get the whole idea of juicing.

In this case peel the ginger, beet (or buy already prepared and ready to use), carrots, pineapple, and cucumbers.

Next cut and chop the fruits and veggies.

Put all the fruits and veggies from the ingredients list into your favorite juicer or blender or a combination of juicer/blender (Nutribullet) and strictly follow the directions of the manual that comes with your machine.

The manual that comes with your machine will tell you what buttons to push and what speed to use.

Juice the softer textures first.

You will see that when you are juicing the crunchier veggies and fruits they will help you push the softer and more delicate fruits and veggies through the blades.

Juice and blend all the ingredients from the list above together as per instructions.

You can always add some raw honey or sweatener depending on your goal with these juices. If the juice is too strong for you, you might also add some ice cubes or source water.

Enjoy the delicious Exotic Strawberry Rasperry Vitality Drink!

Natural Purple Energy Miracle

1 handful of kale
2 handful of baby spinach
6 stalks of celery
3 spray of parsley
1 lemon
1 lime
1/2 bulb of fennel
1 beet
3 carrots
1 juicy apple
1 small cucumber

The ingredients of the Natural Purple Vitality Miracle are all very beneficial for the body and brain.

The secret combination lies in the mix of red and green ingredients.

The beetroot is one of the most healthy vegetables on earth. Consuming beets will help you feel energized. Beets are great for nourishing your brain. It can assist in lowering blood pressure.

Beets contain a very broad amount of minerals and vitamins. Add some beets to your juices to instantly up and power pack your nutrients without adding more calories or fat.

Beet juices are highly nutritious. Beet contains a number of essential minerals and vitamines: Folate, Potassium, Manganese, Dietary Fiber, Vitamine C, Iron, Copper, Phoshorus and Magnesium.

Beet juice is a powerful blood cleanser. Beet contains nutrients that protect against heart diseases, as well as certain types of cancer - particularly colon cancer.

The pigment of beet that is responsible for the deep red purple color of beets is a natural cancer fighting agent. It is called betacyanin. Patients who are treated for stomach cancer, beet juice has been identified and found to have critical influence, inhibiting the cancer cell mutations.

The B vitamin folate aids in tissue growth.

The alkaline Kale combined with the beets makes an unbeatable juice cocktail that helps you reenergize and rejuvenate at the same time. I enjoy one of these whenever my energy levels are down and this is a true vitality booster!

The Natural Purple Energy Miracle contains the following ingredients:

Ingredients:

1 handful of kale (organic if possible)
2 handful of baby spinach (organic if possible)
6 stalks of celery (organic if possible)
3 spray of parsley (organic if possible)
1 lemon (organic if possible)
1 lime (organic if possible)
½ bulb of fennel (organic if possible)
1 beet (organic if possible) plus the beet leaves from 1 beet
3 carrots (organic if possible)
1 juicy apple (organic if possible)
1 small cucumber (organic if possible)

Directions:

For all these juice recipe For the directions please refer to the chapter where I am talking about my 5 Minute 6 Step Juicing System.

Here is a short instruction that sums up what to do. Make sure to refer back to my 6 step process for juicing so that you get the whole idea of juicing.

Be sure to peel the apple, beet, cucumber, lemon, lime, and carrots. Scrub the carrots if they are organic. If not organic, peel the skin to eliminate the risk of pesticides. Wash all fruits and vegetables carefully before the juicing process.

Next cut and chop the fruits and veggies.

Put all the fruits and veggies from the ingredients list into your favorite juicer or blender or a combination of juicer/blender (Nutribullet) and strictly follow the directions of the manual that comes with your machine.

The manual will tell you what buttons to push and what speed to use.

Juice the softer textures first.

You will see that when you are juicing the crunchier veggies and fruits they will help you push the softer and more delicate fruits and veggies through the blades.

If you are not using a juicer and only have a blender available, make sure to first strain the juice from the lemon and lime.

Once it is finished you can either leave the pulp inside or take it out. This is totally up to your preference.

In this case you have to add the juice back to the blender and proceed from there.

Juice and Blend the juices with the other ingredients from the list above together as per instructions.

You can always add some raw honey or sweatener depending on your goal with these juices. If the juice is too strong for you, you might also add some ice cubes or source water.

Enjoy your Natural Purple Vitality Miracle!

Juicing For Vitality & Energy The Smart Way

These are some pro tips you can apply to these healthy smoothies to make your juicing habits even more effective:

1. Balance fruits and veggies because they are easier to eat on the run. In general, people eat more fruits than vegetables. When you are juicing, make sure to strive for a ratio of at least three parts of veggies and one part of fruits. This will help you to take in veggies while keeping your total sugar content under control.

2. Sweeten up your drink. Hearty greens like kale, beets, parsley and swiss chard, are bitter in taste and it helps to add some fruits like apples to sweeten up your juice. You can also try a spice like cinnamon or allspice.

If that is still not enough, drizzle a few drops of honey or maple syrup into your juice.

3. Drink your juice promptly. It is best to enjoy it immediately after the juicing process otherwise you will lose nutrients. Damage and loss or nutrients starts as soon as the drink is exposed to oxygen.

Just think about how quickly a slice of avocado or apple starts to get brown! It is therefore best to consume your juice no longer than 15 minutes after the juice is in your glass.

If you are preparing the juice for later make sure to store it for a short period of time in a mason jar with a very tight seal.

4. Never gulp down your juice, but drink it with the philosophy of mindfulness.

Chewing" and Swishing the liquid before swallowing helps you with the digestion process. It also maximizes both satiety and assimilation.

5. Make sure to maintain quality control because you only want to stick to organic fruits and vegetables. You have to be aware that juicing does require a bigger amount of veggies and fruits than if you were just eating the same amount

Only use the most nutritious veggie and fruit varieties that you can find and concentrate on vegetables and fruits that are higher in beta-carotene and minerals than others. Always include veggies like cabbage, kale, romaine, and celery.

6. Never waste the plant parts of the veggies. The bases of broccoli and cauliflower and asparagus can be used for juicing. The stems and the leaves of beets are perfect for juicing, too.

7. The right tools can save you lots of time. Always make sure to look for a juicer that has a wide mouth. A mouth that is able to eject the pulp and that is easier to clean.

Having a fast juicer can make the difference between you enjoying juicing every day and you not enjoying juicing at all and quitting the whole idea of juicing.

This is why buying a quality juicer is critical for your whole juicing success.

8. As for blenders, keep in mind that blenders are not juicers. It is good to have a juicer and a blender, but keep in mind that blenders simply cannot make juices.

In addition to your daily juicing habits, keep eating whole natural foods, too, because juices alone are not enough.

You want to take in whole natural and organic foods

9. I encourage you to drink your Secret Morning Elexir, then your first morning juice and/or smoothie (depending on your goal) and eat whole foods on a daily basis.

Like this you make sure that you provide your body with a great nutrition, a high amount of fibers that comes from the whole foods as well as a complementary intake of micronutrients.

Power Up Your Juicing Habits With Healing & Detoxifiying Wheat Grass Elixirs

Wheat grass is simply put a young wheat plant. Wheat grass is widely consumed in liquid form by health conscious people who prefer the concentrated rich source of enzymes, minerals and vitamins.

The main aspect that makes these wheat grass juices so healthy is the fact that it contains chlorophyll.

Nearly 70% of wheat grass is chlorophyll. Some individual state that a small pound of wheat grass is equal to 20 pounds of fresh garden greens! This is just one of the reason why health fans are liquefying this grass and drinking it.

Wheat grass juice is quickly rising to the top of the favorite juices.

It retains most of the essential minerals. These minearls, enzymes and vitamins are promoting health and help repair cell damage.

Wheat grass juice also has the ability to increase oxygenation in the human body plus it helps build up the red blood cells. These red blood cells are the carriers of oxygen to the body's cells. In addition it purifies our blood and organs while destroying the nasty toxins. In general, wheat grass is a true metabolism booster.

Wheat grass juice is the perfect replacement for dark green leafy vegetables that you should supplement your diet with.

Wheatgrass is also a very rich source of alkalinity for the body. It is often found in supplemental form so that you can mix it with water and drink it if you do not have an adequate juicer that can process wheat grass. Some fans choose to drink a daily glass of fresh wheatgrass juice to insure that their body is getting enough alkaline forming food.

Juicers can break down the cellulose barriers and extract all of the juice inside fruits, grasses and veggies.

However, you should know that not all juicers are capable of making real wheat grass juice.

If you try to juice wheat grass in a juicer that is not made to process grass, you will probably end up with a damaged or clogged juicer.

The best juicers for wheat grass are those that are multipurpose juicers. These multipurpose juicers will not only make juices from veggies and fruits, but you can apply them to make wheat grass.

If you have any questions, simply ask lots of questions before buying your juicer.

You may want to purchase a wheat grass juicer if you plan to only process grass. These juicers are also known as single auger juicers. They are crushing the grass while squeezing out all of the rich chlorophyll juice of the grass.

Newer models of these single auger juicers do include two levels. The first level works to crush the grass and squeeze out the healthy juice while the second level pulls the remaining pulp through a second crushing and extraction process.

Today you can find many models of these auger or juice extractors. Do not let buying a juicer get in your way. Simply identify what type of juicer you want by determining what type of ingredients you want to process.

Remember, when you get into the habit of drinking healthy wheat grass juice, you should go step by step and start out slowly because the taste of the wheat juice migh surprise you at first.

I did not like the taste at all when I got started, but learned how to integrate these healthy green juices into my daily juicing ritual.

I started by drinking one ounce per day and slowly work my way up to three ounces per day which is ther perfect amount in order to get the most nutritious value into the system of the body.

You will see that such a habit will bring long term health and a clean and lean body!

Juicing For Vitality & Energy Quiz

Juicing For Vitality

T	V	Q	Y	Q	X	N	U	A	F	Q	K	U	H
W	B	E	E	T	P	I	N	E	A	P	P	L	E
L	M	I	P	P	N	G	A	R	L	I	C	V	O
L	A	N	R	A	D	I	S	H	A	J	N	P	V
B	L	Y	L	A	I	N	D	K	A	L	E	P	B
P	W	R	S	P	I	N	A	C	H	J	J	E	K
M	U	E	U	S	N	A	P	P	L	E	O	R	I
E	O	X	U	E	R	K	M	J	E	M	L	Q	N
I	G	G	L	E	M	O	N	N	P	O	F	M	M
T	C	A	R	R	O	T	S	L	M	A	R	R	P
M	G	I	N	G	E	R	Q	B	I	A	A	M	Q
E	J	A	K	S	T	O	M	A	T	O	E	D	E
R	A	S	P	E	R	R	I	E	S	D	R	W	Y
Y	C	D	M	M	Q	T	U	Y	X	V	W	F	A

And Energy

All you have to do is find 12 juicing ingredient related words. Use your imagination, read backwards, sidewards, and forwards to find the correct Juicing related words and associations. Go to the next page to see the correct answers!

Have fun:)

Answers

Quiz Answers:
1. Lemon
2. Ginger
3. Apple
4. Pineapple
5. Spinach
6. Carrots
7. Kale
8. Rasperries
9. Tomatoe
10. Beet
11. Garlic
12. Radish

Conclusion

I have a lot of fun experimenting with these juicing recipes and I hope that these same recipes are getting you started with your own vitality and energy juicing goals, too.

There's a lot of satisfaction when you stumble on a healthy juicing recipe that tastes fantastic, too. It's even more gratifying if the recipe is 5 minute quick and simple to make at the same time.

Don't be afraid to add or remove ingredients to make the recipe your own and as Ann Wigmore, one of the front-runners of today's raw food movement, declared, "Be creative; you just need to understand approximately what to do."

When you do make changes, jot them down! There is little worse than playing around and making a great recipe only to realise you can't remember precisely what you probably did. By making juices that you adore, you'll find yourself anticipating your juice breakfast or juice break.

Since they're so high in nourishment, you will begin to feel more fit.

If you're like me, you may also find that the more that you drink juices, the more that you will begin to enjoy healthier food options like salads and fresh items. Convenience foods like potato chips will begin to taste tasteless.

The additional energy you get from the fruit, vegetable and plant based juices will also assist you in working out more.

All this will assist you in making your juicing efforts a big success!

I attempted to make this Juicing For Vitality & Energy system as easy, fascinating, inspiring, easy to use and as practical to consume as possible for you because a system like this has to be compatible with today's fast paced and mobile world.

Just keep the book on your portable gadget next to your working table and go through one recipe at a time and as you progress with your own juicing goals for health, vitality and energy.

Make it a fun and exciting challenge and stick to it. Remember changing your eating and drinking habits is becoming easier and easier as time goes by and as you get used to your new juicing habits. This is a marathon and not a sprint. It is important to take your time in order to change your habits, improve, and adapt to this new juicing lifestyle!

The book is intended to be used in an interactive and stimulating fashion and to empower you to take action at the same time.

Remember the juices are 5 minute quick to prepare so this even works for the busiest person in the world.

Ultimately, the goal of this book is to lead you to a healthy lifestyle that includes healthy and nutritious juices and food choices.

Including these healthy juicing drinks into your daily meal plans and including them into your lifestyle is what you should be aiming for as your ultimate goal.

Once you are at the level of including healthy juices into your daily lifestyle, you have achieved a big success towards a healthy lifestyle because your body uses the natural healing power of these plant based foods and superfoods that are contained in these juices.

Your body will be able to provide protection and fight infections and viruses. It will be able to heal itself, boost your vitality and energy and utlimately safe you from lots of pain, diseases and expensive doctor bills.

This is a goal that you will never be able to achieve with some common food alternatives or fancy meal plans. Following the latest food trends that are popular is a plan for error and disaster and you do not want to be a victim of these chemically, sick making, and industrially fabricated food design products..

The plan of this Juicing for vitality and energy lifestyle, however, is very kind and intelligent because it follows the rules and the creativity of the nature and the body. It nurishes and energizes the body throughout the day with all the beneficial ingredients and nutrients that are beneficial for the body and mind and it keeps your body and mind productive all the time.

I hope you will use and consume the content whenever you need some inspiration and motivation for making some healthy juice drinks that are helping you live the healthy lifestyle.

Remember, all you have to do is open the book and start with the first juice drink preparation.

Go through all of them and apply them on a daily basis as you see fit and depending on the health goal that you are looking to achieve.

Remember to get started every morning with the Secret Morning Elixir first before drinking your first juice in order to accelerate the health benefits that come with juicing.

You will soon see for yourself that making these juices is a lot of fun plus a lifestyle with juices is going to make you very happy, satisfied, balanced, fit, and energized!

Double your vitality, energy, and life today by the power of juicing!

To your success!

Did you love *Juicing Recipes Book For Vitality, Energy, Health And Fitness Nutrition 14 Healthy Clean Eating & Drinking Juice Cleanse Recipes*? Then you should read *Fasting Book For Health, Fitness, Weight Loss & Detoxing 11 Juicing For Beginners Recipes With delicious & Healthy Fruit & Vegetable Juices* by Juliana Baltimoore!

Juliana Baltimoore

Fasting Book For Health, Fitness, Weight Loss & Detoxing 11 Juicing For Beginners Recipes With delicious & Healthy Fruit & Vegetable Juices...Using a combination of these delicious healthy low calorie juicing recipes from this collection plus following a strict 2 month Juicing diet with the juicing recipes that are included in this book, the author has been able to lose 40 lbs over two months. She has been able to stick to healthy juices after her juicing diet and this change of habit has helped her develop and maintain a lean body and a clear mind. Inside you will learn what juicing can do for you. There is an unlimited array of health benefits of juicing and Juicing to loose weight is one aspect of juicing. Inside this book Juliana will focus on juicing to loose weight and show you exactly how she lost 40 lbs in 60 days, but here are some more powerful benefits that you might consider about the power of getting yourself into a juicing habit: Applying a daily juicing ritual will not only make your body lean, it will also provide your body with unlimited health benefits. These are just some of the health benefits that come with a daily juicing ritual. There is truly an unlimited amount of health benefits that comes with juicing. Here are the most important ones: Weight Loss Antioxidants Alzheimer's Prevention Asthma Help (I suffered for years from breathing problems and Asthma and finally was able to get rid of it because of my daily Juicing and Smoothie ritual) Blood Cleanse Arthritis Prevention Bone Protection Cancer Prevention Cervical Cancer Prevention Breast Cancer Prevention Colon Cancer Prevention Liver Cancer Prevention Lung Cancer Prevention Prostate Cancer Prevention Cataracts Prevention Ovarian Cancer Prevention Stomach Cancer Prevention Digestion Detoxification Energy Digestion Heart Disease Prevention Immune System Hydration Improving Eyesight Improved Complexion Increased Blood Circulation Kidney Cleanse Increased Libido Liver Cleanse Lower Blood Pressure Lower Cholesterol Macular Degeneration Prevention Mental Health Osteoporosis Prevention Pain Relief Reduce Inflammation Reduce Water Retention Stroke Prevention and an unlimited amount of other health benefits. Juicing is a simple to acquire skill and if you turn this skill into a habit, you will be able to live a health, fit, clean, toxin free and lean life from the inside out and for a very long time. Juicing keeps the doctor away and doubles your life! See you inside where you will discover the power of juicing to loose weight. Follow these amazing juicing vegetables, juicing fruits, juicing alkaline, juicing raw & juicing paleo juicing to loose weight recipes, 5 minute quick to make and delicious fat burning juices & weight loss blender juice recipes today and keep the doctor away...this juicing ritual will double your happiness and health so get started today...

About the Publisher

InfinitYou is a hybrid general interest trade publisher. One of the first of its kind InfinitYou publishes physical books, electronic books, and audiobooks in various genres. Our publications are meant to educate, edify and entertain readers of all walks of life from babies to the elderly. Home to more than twenty imprints such as Infinit Baby, Infinit Kids, Infinit Girl, Infinit Boy, Infinit Coloring, Infinit Swear Words, Infinit Activities, Infinit Productivity, Infinit Cat, Infinit Dog, Infinit Love, Infinit Family, Infinit Survival, Infinit Health, Infinit Beauty, Infinit Spirituality, Infinit Lifestyle, Infinit Wealth, Infinit Romance, and lots more.

www.ingramcontent.com/pod-product-compliance
Lightning Source LLC
LaVergne TN
LVHW020431080526
838202LV00055B/5136